Aren't You Glad Jesus Asked?

12 QUESTIONS OUR LORD ASKS
THOSE WHO FOLLOW HIM

FRANK GREGORY

Stay Linda, Focused on Jesus.

Frank Gregory

IS. 57:10

Aren't You Glad Jesus Asked?

12 QUESTIONS OUR LORD ASKS THOSE WHO FOLLOW HIM

FRANK GREGORY

Randall House

PUBLICATIONS • WORLDWIDE MINISTRIES

114 Bush Road • PO Box 17306
Nashville, Tennessee 37217 USA

randallhouse.com

Aren't You Glad Jesus Asked?
12 Questions Our Lord Asks Those Who Follow Him

by Frank Gregory

© Copyright 2003
Randall House Publications

All scripture quotations, unless otherwise indicated, are taken from the HOLY BIBLE, NEW INTERNATIONAL VERSION®. NIV®. Copyright ©1973, 1978, 1984 by International Bible Society. Used by permission of Zondervan. All rights reserved.

Printed in the United States of America

ISBN: 0-89265-541-0

CONTENTS

$\mathscr{D}$EDICATION

❦

SHE sits alone in her house.

She will be 75 years old this fall and has never owned an automobile. Her life is simple, yet has influenced the complicated lives of many others.

By the time she was barely 50 years of age, both her parents, her husband, and two of her children had died; but she refused to become bitter.

She is my mother, Pearl Gregory. She has been known as "Mom" to a lot more kids than just her seven children and "Mema" to multitudes besides her twelve grandchildren. She is my hero.

I love you, Mom; and it is with every ounce of love and appreciation I possess that I dedicate this book to you.

FORWARD

❧

With hundreds of books available on evangelism, do we need another one? The answer is a resounding "yes," if that book is biblically and theologically sound, and if it gives genuine practical help in witnessing, not simply ivory-tower theory.

Aren't You Glad Jesus Asked? passes those tests wonderfully. Written out of a burden to reach people with the gospel, this book is a welcome edition to other resources in the field of evangelism. It is simple enough to be used by a beginner in witnessing, but deep enough to challenge those who have practiced evangelism for years.

The first strong feature of the book is its Christ-centered focus. The gospel is all about Christ, and one cannot read this book without being pointed to Him again and again. As Jesus says in John 12:32, *"If I be lifted up, I will draw all persons to Me."* This book lifts up Christ.

Second, this book is biblical. The author recognizes that the most effective means of evangelism is setting forth the life-changing message of the Scriptures. This book does not just refer to biblical passages, it explains them and applies them. God's Word, combined with the ministry of the Holy Spirit, brings conviction of sin, and points us to the only solution to our sin problem—a personal relationship with Jesus Christ.

Third, this book is practical. I have known Frank Gregory for years, and have seen first-hand his heart for people and passion for evangelism. He does not write as a theoretician, but as a practitioner. His zeal and competency in evangelism resound throughout this book.

I have taught in my personal evangelism classes for years that one of the most neglected skills in evangelism training is the ability to listen. I encourage my students to "ask good questions and then listen, listen, listen." As we listen we will determine where persons are in their understanding, in what or whom they are trusting, and how to best communicate the love of Christ with them.

Frank Gregory has given us a wonderful tool to ask questions. Utilizing the format of Jesus' questions (and answers), he sets forth numerous beautiful pictures of God's amazing grace. I believe this approach will find great reception in the hearts and minds of people of this generation. Jesus touched people who were hurting and confused in His day. People reflect those same needs today, and Jesus still longs to touch them. What better way to communicate the Savior's love than through His own words?

Finally, Frank reminds us of the importance of telling the good news. His approach does not negate the verbal sharing of the good news of Jesus' death for sinners, and of His burial and resurrection that we might share in His power. Frank understands that the priority of our lives should reflect that of our Savior: *"to seek and save the lost"* (Luke 19:10). That is why this book is so pertinent. It not only reminds us of our calling to witness for Christ, it also gives us practical help in doing so.

FORWARD

❧

I heartily commend this book to you for your own edification and for use in sharing Christ with others. May all who read it be able to answer the question, "But who do YOU say that I am?" with "You are the Christ, the son of the living God."

Dr. Timothy Beougher
Professor of Evangelism, Southern Baptist Theological Seminary, Louisville, Kentucky
June 2003

꙳

DO you and I really care about what other people are thinking? Are we so busy formulating what we are going to say next that we don't listen to what other people are saying? Do we even know the right questions to ask someone who is hurting?

Jesus knew more than any man who ever walked the earth; yet He was not afraid to ask questions. He asked many questions, many more, I am convinced than are actually recorded. The questions we do have access to, though, give us great insight into the "mind of Christ."

Having the mind of Christ means thinking like He thought. Jesus definitely thought along the lines of question-asking.

Question-asking has almost become a lost art. What has caused this brilliant form of communication to almost go extinct? The biggest obstacle is our pride. We do not want to appear weak by asking questions. The Western way of thinking lends itself to tell, tell, tell rather than to ask, ask, ask.

This way of thinking has infiltrated the church and even our methods of evangelism. In other words, we are a whole lot better at telling people how bad they are, rather than asking how we can pray for them.

The purpose of this book is to help us realize just how many questions Jesus asked in His approach at teaching us how to live. It is believed that Jesus' earthly father, Joseph, studied at a rabbinical school where question-asking was the main thrust of the teaching methods. If this is true, there is no doubt that Jesus was heavily influenced by this in His formative years.

It is my prayer that several things will happen to you as you read through this book:

1. That you will gain a greater love and appreciation for Jesus.

2. That you will see the tremendous relevance of the questions Jesus asked.

3. That you will be challenged to begin doing a lot more asking and a lot less telling.

There are desperate and dying people out there. May God give us the wisdom to approach them with the grace and truth that Jesus did.

CHAPTER
1

WOMAN,
WHY
ARE YOU
CRYING?

CHAPTER 1

❧

WOMEN are a magnificent work of God. Their outer beauty turns our heads but their inner beauty captures our hearts. A strong, determined woman is a thing of beauty.

As I write this chapter, I am surrounded by pictures of the most important ladies in my life. On the wall is an e-mail photo of my mother. On my desk is a picture of my three daughters and on one of my end tables is a picture of my lovely wife, Becky.

I do not profess to be an expert on the subject of women, but I have had a fair amount of exposure to them. Being the only boy in the family with four sisters, the process is repeating itself with my three daughters.

Since my father died when I was only nine, I have spent the bulk of my life in a female dominated environment. I am closely surrounded by nine females (wife, mother, three daughters, four sisters) and I love it. I do not know if there is an expert on women, but at the age of 50, I can just about go toe to toe with any man about women. Maybe that is why this question so captured my heart.

It is the first day of the week and women are going to the tomb of Jesus to anoint His body. It is interesting that so many women loved Jesus in a non-sensual way. He drew their affection even in His death.

Upon arriving at the tomb, they find His body is not there. Fear and panic strike their hearts as they come to the realization that someone has stolen the body of Jesus.

They immediately go and tell the disciples. Once again the women have to tell the men what is going on. The disciples go to investigate. Remember, if I say it, you doubt it; if you say it, it's true.

They find an empty tomb just as Mary has said. Content that Mary had told the truth, Peter and John leave, still trying to rationalize what has happened these past three days. Mary, though, stays behind not knowing what to do. She just wants to find Jesus. In certain frustration and possibly even desperation, Mary does what most women do at this point. She crys. Hence the question, "Woman, why are you crying?"

It is true that women cry more than men. This does not mean they are emotionally weaker; it just means they are less inhibited about showing their emotions and crying happens to be one of them. Crying in and of itself is not wrong. It is a very natural reaction to the despair Mary was feeling. Let's look at the characters involved in this scene as John recorded it (John 20:1-18).

Mary of Magdala also known as Mary Magdalene had followed Jesus for some time. She was a product of demon exorcism and had helped to support the ministry of Jesus and the apostles. Her deep devotion to Jesus is made evident here in that she feared no arrest or persecution in light of visiting the burial place of Jesus.

The angels were there to give the message of hope to those who came looking for a body. At this particular time, however, they posed the question to Mary that Jesus would also ask. The question asked exactly the same way twice was rhetorical in nature. The angels knew why Mary was crying and they no doubt knew her name, but, nonetheless, they made the question generic.

Notice how Mary answered the angels. "They have taken my Lord away and I don't know where they have put Him." Mary was crying because they had taken away her reason for living! Jesus had changed her life and she was broken not only over His death, but, also, over His body supposedly being stolen.

At this point she turns and sees Jesus but she does not realize that it is He. He then asks her exactly what the angels asked and adds another question.

"Woman, why are you crying?" Jesus knew whom He was addressing. I believe He used the noun "woman" instead of the name Mary for some very specific reasons.

Jesus not only asked Mary this question but also every woman who has ever cried. Millions of women are still crying.

A single mother cries because she fears she and her children may not be able to survive financially another year. An abandoned wife cries because she is the victim of an unfaithful husband's unbridled lust. A beaten wife cries not just because of the physical pain she feels but also because of the emotional scars heaped upon her by a man who promised to honor her. A teenage girl cries every time she sees a baby because she cannot escape the life she ended that resulted from a night of misdirected passion. A mother who hasn't heard from her drug addicted son in months weeps because she does not know if he is still alive. Jesus asks you, "Woman, why are you weeping?"

Jesus did not reprimand Mary for crying and He will not reprimand you even though much of your crying is unnecessary. His first question is actually answered in His second one, "Who is it you are looking for?"

Jesus knew Mary's crying was needless because He was not missing. He still asks women today what they are looking for. So many women are still looking for "Mr. Right" or a "Knight on the white horse" to come along and sweep them off their feet. No one will fulfill your need for a relationship like Jesus. Nothing else will substitute for the love, acceptance, dignity, and worth that Jesus can give you.

Mary deeply loved Jesus because He had delivered her from the demons of her past. Mary loved Jesus because he looked into her eyes when He spoke to her and did not scan the rest of her body. Stop waiting on one person to meet all your needs because that person does not exist. Only Jesus can bring restoration to your soul.

When asked whom she was looking for, Mary answered by referring to Jesus with a pronoun assuming He was already part of the conversation. "Sir, if you have carried Him away, tell me where you have put Him and I will get Him." Notice the sincerity in her reply. She did not sarcastically answer in a way that would make anyone not want to help her. She, like so many women, was desperately looking for Jesus.

CHAPTER 1

⁂

Then came one of the most chilling moments in human history. Jesus says her name. This is so awesome. Jesus begins the conversation in a very general way and then brings it to a personal climax. When Jesus said Mary's name she knew immediately who He was. All the casting, music, and lighting of a major production could not capture the drama of that moment.

John tells us that Mary turned toward Jesus and cried out "Rabboni!" (which means teacher). Jesus calls the names of many women who are crying. Kimberly, Betty, Melba, Dana, why are you crying? Jesus wants you to do what Mary did, turn to Him and acknowledge Him as Lord and Savior.

Jesus Christ has risen from the dead. He stands at your door and calls your name.

Mary was never the same again. Jesus had changed her life forever. He does not want you to weep needlessly. He wants you to know there is hope.

QUESTIONS

1. Jesus lived in a "man's world." Why did He bother with women?

2. What other women possibly influenced Jesus besides His own mother?

3. Was Mary crying only because she thought Jesus' body had been stolen?

4. God chose shepherds to tell of Jesus' birth. He chose women to tell of the resurrection. Neither group had much of a voice in society. Why did God choose them?

5. Why didn't Mary recognize Jesus?

6. In what ways was Mary representative of women for generations to come?

7. Do you think Mary ever cried again about Jesus dying?

8. Describe the feelings you have standing at the grave of a loved one.

9. What should be the point of your crying?

10. Discuss how Mary's reason for crying was actually the hope of the world.

Chapter 2

WHO
TOUCHED
MY
CLOTHES?

CHAPTER 2

❧

OH, the power of touch. It has the ability to make lasting impressions—some good, some not so good. Touch helps us to know where we stand in a relationship. A business deal is sealed by a handshake, children long to feel an approving pat on the head from their father, a player is encouraged by a slap on the back from a coach, and the hearts of young romantics skip several beats when they hold hands for the first time.

While I attended Wheaton College Graduate School I worked in the warehouse at Scripture Press Publications. The wife of one of the guys I worked with was expecting their first baby. The two ladies who worked in the warehouse decided we should give Matt a baby shower.

It was definitely a unique baby shower. The men outnumbered the women nearly 10 to 1. It was also the first baby shower most of us men had ever attended. One of the ladies decided we would end the shower by each of us giving Matt one word of parental advice. This was also interesting since several of the young men in attendance had no children.

My advice was profound. I told Matt to make sure he left for the hospital on time (our third child Tiffany was born only eight minutes after arriving at the hospital). The only other advice given to Matt that I remember was from one of the supervisors named Rod. "When he does good, pat him on the back; when he does not so good, go lower down and hit a little harder!"

Who touched my clothes?

I thank God for every way I was touched by my parents, which eventually all made a positive "impact." Touch is very powerful in the nurturing of young children. Babies can die from the lack of touch. It is interesting that we never outgrow our need for touch.

Our society has become so perverted that proper touching is seldom practiced. This has actually added greater value to appropriate touch. Everyone still needs to be touched in appropriate ways. We could all wear the sticker every day that says, "I need a hug."

We, however, in this part of the world are known to be people of the high tech, low touch mindset who really guard our own space. The whole concept of space is revealing in our posturing whether standing or sitting. Have you ever noticed how people mark their territory in places like an airport terminal? We will usually sit in one seat and put something on the seats to our right and left like a book, bag, or briefcase. We are telling everyone else to keep their distance!

Our first line of defense is to prevent anything attached to our person such as clothing, from being touched. Our second line of defense is to prevent our body from being touched, whether that be our clothes or exposed skin. Our third line of defense is not to allow our heads to be touched, such as our face and hair. Someone had better have permission before touching us from the neck up. The head is one of the most intimate places of touch on the human body. You are probably asking what this has to do

❦

with the question at hand. We must realize that the woman in this story broke the cultural mores and committed the taboo of society by touching a man she did not even know.

This fascinating story really was not supposed to have even happened. This is a parenthetical event inserted inside another story—the story of Jesus going to help a sick girl. We find the woman at this time of her life in a definite state of desperation. She was probably depressed as well.

She was physically sick. It is not certain what disease she was suffering from, but the medical profession of her day had probably made it worse. It appears that she had some sort of rare hemorrhaging and was being used as a lab rat by doctors who could not cure her but were just experimenting on her. The medical profession believed for hundreds of years that bleeding someone could cure every disorder from flu to mental illness. George Washington's death was expedited because physicians bled him. It took medical science centuries to discover what Leviticus 17:11 said, "The life is in the blood." No one had been able to stop her bleeding. Remember, these were the days before shots and antibiotics were used, so many medical practices were crude to say the least. Certainly, this woman knew what physical pain was.

She was financially destitute. This woman may have once been a woman of means, but now had been driven to the point of poverty by spending all the money she had trying to restore her health. Good health is a priceless commodity and we will do what we can to have it. Few things drain our bank account faster than a trip to the doctor, followed by a run to the pharmacy.

I believe this woman was emotionally drained. She could have even been suicidal. All hope was gone until she heard about Jesus! Sound familiar?

Jesus had just crossed over the Sea of Galilee on His way to Capernaum. He had delivered a demon possessed man, which would make for a full day for anyone except Jesus Christ. He was still on the shore of the lake when Jairus approached Him about his sick daughter. Jesus began to go with Jairus, and this is when the crowd began to press in. Luke used the word crush in his account to describe the intensity of the crowd's pressure.

This woman, who remained anonymous, had tremendous tenacity. Jesus was attempting to make His way through the crowd. When we are trying to get through large crowds at places like sporting events, amusement parks, or concerts, we usually let down our first two lines of defense because we know we are going to be pushed and prodded by the crowd. So to be touched in this way, in that situation, was no big deal. This is how I believe Jesus was being touched, as the center of attention. When we are in a mass of humanity, we just try to get out. Can you imagine trying to get to someone and fighting against the press of the crowd to do it? This was what this weak woman was up against. What a determined woman! She somehow fought through the crowd and touched Jesus' cloak. A cloak was similar to a coat or jacket. This woman's faith did not even require her to touch Jesus, only something attached to His person. When Jesus asked the question, "Who touched my clothes?" (Mark 5:30), the disciples once again thought He was in mental overload from His previous demoniac encounter. Possibly hundreds of people were touching Jesus; this woman was the only one who touched Him with purpose!

How could any of us let Jesus walk by and not desire to let Him change our lives? With one touch of Jesus' cloak, this woman's life was changed forever.

Her story does not end here. Jesus requires that she make a public profession. Only Jesus and the woman knew what the intention of His question was. He wanted this woman to acknowledge, before the crowd, how He had brought wholeness back to her life.

This woman was afraid because it was not culturally acceptable for her to touch a man in public. Isn't it interesting how many women felt drawn to Jesus and even compelled to touch Him, knowing it could even mean punishment for them? Despite her fears, this woman gives a full-blown testimony to the power of Jesus. Jesus brought calm release to her spirit by saying, "Daughter, your faith has healed you. Go in peace and be freed from your suffering" (Mark 5:34). This woman was willing to fight through the crowd of unbelief, social ridicule, and religious tradition to get to Jesus. What are you willing to do? The question is really not when have you touched Jesus, but when has Jesus touched you? His touch always has the power to change.

QUESTIONS

1. Describe how you think this woman had suffered.

2. Was it possible that Jesus was coming her way, only to change directions thus making it harder for her to get to Him?

3. What makes this anonymous woman's story so powerful?

4. How is touch here in this story more powerful than the spoken word?

✿

5. Why did Jesus still confront the woman after she had touched Him?

6. What signals do we give that say "Do not touch"?

7. Why is it so important for us to touch someone?

8. Share times you have been driven through desperation to do something out of character.

9. Can you relate to this woman?

10. Describe how Jesus is still "touching" lives.

CHAPTER

3

WHY
ARE YOU
BOTHERING
HER

❧

I STOOD with what I am sure was a momentary look of horror on my face. I had not prepared myself for what I was seeing. A young man, who was surely once a very healthy looking young man, stood in front of me. I was standing in the middle of a convenience store. I was working as a salesman (I could have said national account representative to make it sound more important) for a nationwide distributor of sunglasses. Normally I do not go that far into a store because there is usually someone already behind the counter. It was my job to go into convenience stores wherever I was assigned and set up accounts. I averaged going into 20 stores a day. This particular call, though, left an undying impression on me.

It was mid-morning of a summer day. The store was completely void of customers, which was definitely unusual. I strolled in, looking for the manager; seeing no one immediately, I made my way toward the back of the store where the office was located. I was stopped in my tracks by a friendly male voice saying, "May I help you?" I was already somewhat startled by the voice because I was not expecting to hear anyone from that direction. My mild surprise, however, soon gave way to terror as I turned to look at a living burn victim unlike any I had ever seen. My first instinct was to run out of the store without saying a word. The next few moments were clearly reflexive as I tried to collect myself. I went into my salespitch, asking him if he would be interested in seeing my presentation. He agreed, which gave me more time to gain my composure while I went out to get my sample case.

As I made my presentation, I have to admit that I was much more focused on who was in front of me than the product I was showing. This courageous young man obviously had received countless skin grafts, and the most difficult thing I did by the grace of God was to reach out and touch him by shaking his hand, which contained only partial fingers.

As unsettled as I was in my spirit, I left that store thanking God for what He had allowed me to experience that morning. That one encounter changed my life more than all the sales I made while with the company.

We do not like being around people who are different from us. Whether they are different physically, ethnically, intellectually, or spiritually, we find ourselves knocked out of our comfort zone. Someone who is wealthy makes us ashamed of what we do not have. A poor person makes us feel guilty for what we do have. We despise being in an unfamiliar environment, and in the Western world have been programmed to disdain weakness.

Being around a "weak" person makes us extremely uncomfortable because it reflects our own weaknesses, which are too many for any one human to bear. We find such an incident in Mark 14.

Jesus is sitting and talking with the religious leaders when all of a sudden their little ecclesiastical world is turned upside down. Mary, sister of Martha and Lazarus,

CHAPTER 3

❧

breaks up the party by coming and anointing Jesus' feet with expensive perfume and wiping His feet with her hair.

You really can't blame these guys for being upset since they reflect our own self-centered lives. Have you ever been with someone of importance and not wanted to be disturbed because of how it fed your ego to be around him or her? This is, no doubt, how these men felt when Mary comes in and makes such a scene.

Their response drips with a religious spirit. Their self-righteousness will not allow them to reveal their true reason for being upset by this interruption—having the focus switch from them to Mary. A religious spirit will never be transparent but always hypocritical. These men expressed concern for the poor with Judas leading the charge. "Why wasn't this perfume sold and the money given to the poor?" (John 12:5a). Mark wrote that they rebuked her harshly. Here this woman is bowing at the feet of Jesus in brokenness and worship and these "spiritual giants" are giving her grief for it. Jesus' timing is once again impeccable. He asked the question that exposed the very intent of their hearts and brings conviction to every one of us who has played church. "Leave her alone," Jesus said. "Why are you bothering her? She has done a beautiful thing to me" (Mark 14:6).

Jesus gave the command with more authority than Yosemite Sam ever dreamed of having, saying "Back off!" Jesus actually said, "Leave her alone," but I believe He did it with a tone that got the message across to the disciples, especially Judas. I have a feeling that the rub between Jesus

❧

and Judas was growing by the moment. When Jesus asked the men around Him why they were bothering Mary, He was actually asking them what was bothering them. Why had Mary's action caused such an uproar? What had she done to provoke such a pouncing?

Jesus once again uses an event to teach a lesson. He first states that she has done a beautiful thing to Him. Unfettered worship from a humble heart truly is a beautiful sight. Mary was simply displaying her intense love for her Lord as well as showing deep grief concerning His death which was only days away. Remember this took place during Passion Week, Jesus' last week on earth. This particular event probably occurred less than 48 hours before Jesus' death on the cross.

Jesus also made the observation that this woman had done what she could. The perfume she used, which was called nard, was very expensive.

Now men, when I go to Wal-Mart to buy my lovely wife some perfume for whatever special occasion it may be, I at least try to buy something that is locked away and not just setting on the shelf. This perfume was worth a hundred times more than anything Wal-Mart ever locks away. This woman gave her best to Jesus and was accused of being wasteful. Nothing given to Jesus is ever wasted! The value of the perfume exhibited the tremendous value she placed upon Jesus. How much do we value Jesus?

Jesus then makes a remarkable statement that cannot be misinterpreted. "You will always have the poor among you, but you will not always have me" (John 12:8). Jesus was not implying that we should not help the poor. This was one of the signs that the Messiah had come, the poor had the gospel preached to them. Jesus was trying to illustrate the urgency with which He needed to be worshiped. He was stating that the poor were a constant but His physical presence was not.

Jesus was saying that nothing should supercede our worship of Him, not even helping the poor. How often do we attempt to substitute activity for sitting at Jesus' feet?

According to John, this dinner party was given in honor of Jesus. We need to make Jesus the guest of honor in our meetings. This dinner was not about Mary, the disciples, or anyone else there. It was about Jesus!

When we enter a place of worship with a religious spirit, we are coming in with the improper attitude in which brokenness will make us extremely uncomfortable.

The men were made uneasy because Mary had exposed their own self-righteousness, which was a glaring weakness. People who are broken and humble make those who are trying to appear to be part of the superspiritual elite squirm.

Jesus said the woman would be remembered in every generation throughout history where the gospel was preached. It is interesting that Mary did this not so she would be remembered but so she would not forget Jesus!

Her name was Kay. She came in with a small group from her church. Our congregation was observing a day of

✧

prayer and fasting. We were having one of our prayer meetings during the day when this dispatch of prayer warriors came to pray with us.

There was a time of sharing from the Word followed by prayer. People were asked to pray as the Spirit of God prompted them. When Kay began to pray, Heaven started to open. This woman was praying with brokenness like I had not heard in years, maybe ever. It was a weeping, sobbing, make you shake brokenness that you are not used to hearing in many of our sanitized meetings. I was moved, scared, and grateful all at the same time. For some time a religious spirit had permeated our building and was putting a choke hold on our worship. As Kay began to weep and cry loudly before the Lord, the spirit began to leave. It was glorious!

As we were dismissing our time of prayer, I reached over and took Kay's hand and thanked her for bringing brokenness to our congregation. She again began to weep as we celebrated God's mercy. Our sanctuary has not been the same since.

Why are we put out by someone's brokenness? This is a probing question and can best be answered on our knees. If we are put out as these men were, we can be sure Jesus will ask, "Why are you bothering her?"

CHAPTER 3

❧

QUESTIONS

1. What do you think prompted Mary to "break up" such a meeting with her act of worship?

2. Who do you think Judas and the other men represent?

3. What was the estimated value of the perfume that Mary poured on Jesus?

4. What is the significance of Mary pouring the perfume on Jesus' feet?

❦

5. Jesus could have humiliated Mary by rejecting her. Why didn't He?

6. Describe a time someone became so broken that it made you uncomfortable?

7. Why are we so repulsed by brokenness?

8. When is the last time you were knocked out of your comfort zone?

CHAPTER 3

❧

9. How does a religious spirit distract from worship?

10. What urgency was present in Mary's act of worship that is often missing in ours?

CHAPTER

24

WHY
HAVE YOU
FORSAKEN
ME?

IT was December 9, 1971. I walked into the school cafeteria in an unassuming manner with the rest of my fourth grade class. As I stood waiting in line, I noticed two girls from high school looking at me in a somewhat bewildered way. I did what most fourth grade boys do, I forgot about it and went on through the line.

As I sat down to eat, Nan Bull, the school librarian, who was also the superintendent's wife (I attended a small school), came up and asked me if I was hungry. I thought she was taking a survey about the food. I told her I didn't know and she said, "Why don't you just drink your milk and come with me." At this point I thought I was in trouble, but I did not know what I had done.

Mrs. Bull escorted me to a car being driven by Edith Cranford, who would later become a close family friend. It is incredible how the events of such a day stick in your mind. Mrs. Cranford drove a green Pontiac, the school cafeteria was serving meatloaf, and I was wearing a brown shirt with white stripes, blue jeans and black canvas tennis shoes. It was a cold rainy day. Very befitting of what had happened.

I got into Mrs. Cranford's car and found my sister Sammie weeping uncontrollably. I knew something was wrong.

Mrs. Cranford was doing this because her husband Ralph was the town pharmacist. Our family did not have a phone and the hospital had called Ralph to give him the news.

As we pulled into our driveway the yard was already filling up with cars. I knew something really bad was wrong but I still was not expecting the worst. I walked into our living room and looked around at all the people who were staring at me with blank looks. I said, "What's wrong?" My Mom said, "You mean nobody told you?" I said "No." My Mom looked up at me and said "Daddy's dead." I was numb. It felt as though the whole world had collapsed on me. Those two words changed my world and gave me an issue to deal with for almost the next 30 years.

Abandonment is one of the greatest spiritual ills to permeate our culture and can be experienced in many different forms. It involves not only death but also divorce, desertion and what has come to be known as socially accepted neglect. People experience abandonment through the death of a child, parent, sibling, or close friend. Abandonment manifests itself through desertion of a parent either permanently or temporarily. Children who are left for days or even hours by a parent not knowing when they will return live in abandonment.

One of the best biblical descriptions of abandonment is found in Psalm 88:15-18: "From my youth I have been afflicted and close to death; I have suffered your terrors and am in despair. Your wrath has swept over me; your terrors have destroyed me. All day long they surround me like a flood; they have completely engulfed me. You have taken my companions and loved ones from me; the darkness is my closest friend."

❦

Abandonment leaves a feeling of hopelessness, terror, and despair. It is amazing how many people have suffered from abandonment. Marilyn Monroe was a foster child carted from one home to the next. Elvis Presley never recovered from the death of his mother. I have preached messages dealing with this subject at youth camps and have as much fallout from the adult sponsors as I do the kids. Abandonment makes you feel lonely and isolated. You feel as though you are cut off from the mainstream and not good enough to be accepted. It also builds a huge wall between you and your Heavenly Father.

Our culture suffers today from what I call AFS—Absent Father Syndrome. Putting political correctness aside, God is not called our mother though He possesses maternal attributes. He is called "Our Father." The enemy has done a great job of creating anger toward the Heavenly Father through millions of "deadbeat dads" who reside both in and out of the home. The anger that exists among abandoned children is intense. It also gives birth to a lack of self-esteem. The hopelessness can be overwhelming except for the cross.

Thank God for the cross! The cross is the most significant event in human history. It was on the cross that Jesus experienced abandonment for the first time in His life. Just as Jesus was about to die, He asked possibly the most perplexing question He ever asked, "My God, my God, why have you forsaken me?" (Matthew 25:46). This powerful question had several implications. It is the only time that

Jesus addressed His father as "God" and not as "Father." Every other place Jesus referred to God the Father as "my father." God the Father had turned His back on God the Son because the sin of the world had been laid on Jesus and God could not bear to look. No theologian has been able to explain what happened when Jesus' emaciated body was hanging on the cross. He cried, "Why have you forsaken me?" and the Father made no reply. All Heaven must have wept. The most skilled actor could not capture the trauma of that moment. Jesus experienced abandonment for a moment so we would not have to for a lifetime. This is said so accurately in Isaiah 54:7—"For a brief moment I abandoned you, but with deep compassion I will bring you back."

God turned His back but it was not permanent. After Jesus died God stepped on the scene and the result is the empty tomb. Acts 2:26 says "Therefore my heart is glad and my tongue rejoices; my body also will live in hope, because you will not abandon me to the grave, nor will you let your Holy One see decay."

Jesus was not left by His Father in that cold, musty tomb but was brought forth never to be abandoned again! I personally struggled with abandonment for many years and did not even realize it. After my father died when I was nine, I experienced the normal cycle of grief, which included anger, sadness, self-pity, and poor self-esteem. I never saw myself, though, as a victim of abandonment. I thought abandonment applied only to those kids whose moms or dads had run out on them. If you had walked up to me when I was a teenager and said my dad had abandoned me, I would have been on you like white on rice. My father loved me and would have never left me. The fact remained though that my father did leave me, albeit unintentionally.

I always had a very close relationship with my father. We hunted and fished together. I can remember sitting on his lap at the end of the day, scratching my head on his beard. I can still smell his Old Spice cologne. I was his only son of five children and our relationship was special. In the same way, I always had an extremely intimate relationship with my Heavenly Father but something seemed to be missing. I could never fully experience the love and acceptance of Father God. I would pray, fast, and cry out in agony from the depths of my soul and never receive an answer.

My answer came in January 1999, over 27 years after my father's death. I attended a pastors' prayer summit near Tyler, Texas. It was here that I realized how abandonment had been a curse on my life.

The men at the summit were given an opportunity to sit on a chair in the middle of a circle and share their heart. As I shared my heart, God gave the men around me insight into my need for acceptance, having alluded to not having a father to whom I could talk.

As those pastors began to gather around me and lay hands on me to pray, my heart began to melt. I experienced brokenness like I never had in my adult life. They prayed the spirit of abandonment to be taken from me and it was.

By God's grace I fully dealt with my father's death. That evening after my deliverance I stood on the deck of the dining hall as the sun was going down. I looked up into that clear Texas sky and said, "I love you, Dad." I had never told my dad goodbye. He had died suddenly at the age of 42 of a heart condition and there had never been closure. I had also never forgiven him for leaving me—a matter in which he had no choice.

This chapter would have been impossible for me to write five years ago. When confronted with the full impact of my father's death, I chose to receive God's mercy and grace.

Even if you have been abandoned, God loves you and gave His Son so you would not have to live in despair. Psalm 27:10 says, "Though my father and mother forsake me, the Lord will receive me." God put His Son on the cross so you could know love and acceptance. You never have to be alone. The choice is yours. Will you choose the cross?

CHAPTER 4

❦

QUESTIONS

1. Why was the cross the only place Jesus could experience abandonment?

2. Did Jesus know why the Father had abandoned Him?

3. How must God the Father have felt when Jesus asked this question?

4. Why is it significant that there was no answer to Jesus' question?

❧

5. What is the relationship between the darkness that surrounded Jesus and the abandonment He felt?

6. In what ways do people experience abandonment?

7. Is abandonment always intentional?

8. What is the only solution to abandonment?

CHAPTER
5

HOW MANY
LOAVES
DO YOU
HAVE?

❦

I LOVE bread. There are few things like freshly baked bread. Hot biscuits are the crowning touch to a meal of fried chicken, mashed potatoes, gravy, and corn on the cob. It is almost against the law to have a pot of beans and ham without cornbread baked in a cast iron skillet. Hot rolls that have been given proper time to rise complete the turkey dinner on Thanksgiving Day at my mother's.

Bread is the staff of life. Jesus Himself said, "I am the bread of life" (John 6:47). There were many connections made between physical bread and the spiritual bread that Jesus had to offer.

Jesus is in the middle of a teaching conference (Mark 8:1-21) when He is confronted with a food shortage. Can you imagine attending a series of meetings for three days and there are no meals served at all? Unless you were on a fast, you would not consider this a plus to any meeting.

Jesus explains His concern to the disciples by saying, "I have compassion for these people; they already have been with me three days and have nothing to eat. If I send them home hungry, they will collapse on the way, because some of them have come a long distance" (Mark 8:2, 3).

You really have to credit these people with the tenacity they showed along with the hunger they possessed to hear Jesus. In fact, they were so engrossed in Jesus' teaching I think they forgot about even being hungry. Have you ever gone through an emotionally taxing time where your appetite totally left you only to return as you landed with a megaphone declaring "Feed me!" Such was the case with this crowd of four thousand plus.

Jesus was always motivated by compassion. The crowd was physically weak and Jesus was afraid that they would not be able to walk the distance back home (remember this was before cars, bikes, buses, and subways). Jesus presents the challenge to His disciples, which brings us to the truth that Jesus wants us to get involved. Jesus was looking at the issue from the vertical; the disciples were looking at it from the horizontal. They were in the middle of nowhere with no fast food restaurants, no quick stops, and no grocery stores. The question of survival was at hand. Few things bring us closer to our very existence than hunger.

I do not believe the disciples were trying to avoid their responsibilities but they sincerely did not know how they were going to provide food for this mass of people. Even if they had the money to purchase the food, there was nowhere to buy any. They were stumped. They replied to Jesus' request with a question: "But where in this remote place can anyone get enough bread to feed them" (Mark 8:4). Jesus did what He did many times. He answered their question with a question. "How many loaves do you have?" (Mark 8:5a). Jesus asked this question because He desires to use what we have.

One of my daughters' favorite things to do is stop by the convenience store. They love for me to be low on fuel. The low fuel light for them means Slurpees and hot fries. Sometimes when they are enjoying their candy, I will ask

them for a piece of it. They suddenly become very possessive and do not want to share. I am not asking for their
candy because I need it. I do not desire to have their candy
because I do not have the ability to purchase my own. In
fact, I am the one who bought their candy for them. I want
their candy because I want them to share with me.

Jesus does not need what we have. Jesus did not need the
disciples' bread. He could have made all the rocks of the
field turn to bread. Jesus simply wants us to share what we
have with Him. He desires to use it.

In our journey of allowing Jesus to use us we find a principle of utmost importance. Our loaves can never be mul-
tiplied until they are broken. God looks for those who will
become broken before Him.

In this culture of "might makes right" and "only the
strong survive," brokenness is a despised character trait, yet
it is the very characteristic that will get God's attention. My
friend, God is not impressed by our buildings, our tech-
nology, or our abilities. He is, however, drawn to us like a
paper clip to a magnet when we are broken.

Have you allowed God to break you? If you seek to
influence others for Jesus, then you must learn to be broken. Jesus broke the bread and others benefited as their
hunger was satisfied. Jesus was our broken bread of life.

Another principle we learn is that Jesus can do more
with the little we give to Him than the lot we keep for ourselves. We are selfish by nature and do not want to let go.

We are like the disciples; we just do not seem to get it. Jesus asks twice in this narrative, "Do you still not understand?"

This was not the first feeding of the masses the disciples had witnessed. The more familiar feeding of 5,000 had taken place earlier.

This is where the Pharisees step in and demand a sign from Heaven. Get this, the Bread of Life had just fed thousands for the second time with just a few loaves and they are asking for a sign from Heaven. Meanwhile, in the boat Jesus is warning the disciples against the leaven of the Pharisees, meaning their teaching.

Instead of getting what Jesus is saying, the disciples think Jesus is reprimanding them for not bringing enough bread on the boat trip. Do you sense Jesus losing His patience here?

Jesus was trying to communicate with the disciples that even with one loaf of bread He could feed an army. He then begins to ask them how many baskets of bread they picked up after each feeding, showing them that they actually ended up with more bread than they started with each time.

When we give our loaves to Jesus, we always end up with more than we had before. No one can out give God!

Years ago my father-in-law (then my future father-in-law) purchased a set of tires for me. After having the tires put on my car I went to get the front end aligned only to find out my need was much greater than a simple alignment that included a brake job. I made an appointment for

✦

the following Tuesday not knowing where I would get the money.

The next evening my sister, Peggy, came down and helped me to balance my checkbook. We found $100 I did-n't know I had. That Sunday I went and preached to a small congregation in Morrilton, Arkansas. An elderly gentlemen came to me at the close of the evening and handed me a roll of money, probably that day's offering. The night before I was to have my car maintenanced, I was counting what it would cost to have the repairs done and it came to $77.15. I was excited about the $100 my sister had found in my account but I remembered the offering from the congrega-tion the day before. I counted it and was stunned to find that the amount was $77.00. I reached in my pocket to find the only coins there were a dime and a nickel. God met the need to the penny! The next morning I joyfully went to the auto shop and sat and read while the repairs were being made. When the service manager called me to pick up my car he told me it would be $77.15. I put the dime and nick-el on the counter along with the roll of money, mostly ones, and said, "You can count it, it's all there." I did not even have to use the $100 in my checking account until I went back to college that fall! God has met many needs in my life but never like that one to the very last cent.

Jesus was trying to make the disciples see that when their loaves were given to Him, they would never lack anything. He asked them just as He asks us, "Do you still not understand?" Jesus patiently waits for us to bring Him our loaves so that not only we but also others may benefit.

Jesus is asking you, "How many loaves do you have?"

*Q*UESTIONS

1. How can hunger create a mob-like scene?

2. In what way was Jesus trying to get the disciples to think "outside the box"?

3. Was this particular miracle just about satisfying people's hunger?

4. Is the disciples' shortsightedness any different from ours?

CHAPTER 5

❧

5. Why are we possessive toward our Heavenly Father?

6. Why are some people broken while others are not? Is brokenness something we choose?

7. Why are we stuck on seeing the obvious instead of seeing with eyes of faith?

8. How does Jesus bless our lives like He did the bread?

9. What are you allowing Jesus to use so the lives of others can be impacted?

CHAPTER 6

ARE YOU
ENVIOUS
BECAUSE
I AM
GENEROUS?

❧

IT'S bonus time and you are stoked. You are in a high state of anxiety as you open the envelope with this year's check. Your eyes double in size as you read a one with a comma followed by three zeroes. You want to yell "one thousand dollars" but you don't. Your mind begins to race with the possibilities; a pair of mountain bikes, starting that deck on the house, a dinette set, a down payment on a new car—you and your family are ecstatic.

All that excitement, however, is turned into hurt, bitterness, envy and ingratitude just a few days later. You are in the break room discussing bonuses with a co-worker and she "accidentally" lets it slip that her bonus was $1,500 (that's $500 more than yours!). You simply cannot believe your ears. No one has worked harder than you and it is beyond your comprehension that anyone would get a bigger bonus and so you charge into your boss's office to express your feelings of betrayal. Your boss then gently yet firmly reminds you that a bonus is a gift and is not negotiable. It may also be given not strictly on merit but also on need.

Sound familiar? We are all intoxicated with the fairness of life. Everything had better work out to be fair, especially for us.

This truth is never communicated more clearly than in the parable of the vineyard workers. Jesus tells this parable in a response to a question from Peter, "We have left everything to follow you! What then will there be for us?"

❧❧❧

(Matthew 19:27). Not much has changed. Even Jesus was plagued with the age-old question, "What's in it for me?"

The meaning of this parable has been debated and though this chapter is not intended to be an expository explanation, a brief interpretation is necessary if we are to make an adequate attempt to answer the question at hand. I believe Jesus was teaching that God will have the final decision concerning our reception of His riches. We as part of the kingdom experience need to understand that in the market place of life, we are called to God's purpose with God's provision of benefits. It is also essential that we realize that we are not on a merit system, but we operate in the realm of grace.

The landowner of the parable represents God who gives the call to go to work in His vineyard. This is not to advocate that we in any way earn our salvation. We are saved and kept by grace. We are called, however, to labor in the kingdom as a result of being brought into the kingdom. Salvation is more than a fire insurance policy from hell. Our churches have too long been glorified daycare centers with a lot of screaming babies. Instead, we are called to be beachheads and to take territory for the kingdom.

The landowner goes out to the market square at various times of the day to recruit workers: 6:00 A.M., 9:00 A.M., noon, 3:00 P.M., and 5:00 P.M. He reaches an agreement with all the employees regardless of the time they are sent out.

CHAPTER 6

❦

At the end of the day, most likely at 6:00 P.M., all the employees are called in to receive their pay. The landowner begins by paying the ones he hired at 5:00 P.M. Now, remember that these guys have only worked an hour and yet they are receiving a denarius, which was a full days wage. The other men standing around who have worked all day are surely thinking that the landowner had changed his mind and they are going to get more money than was originally agreed upon. After all, how could the boss possibly pay the people who had only worked a partial shift the same as the ones who had pulled a full shift?

The men who worked a full day receive their answer when to their dismay they all received the exact same amount as those who had only worked one hour. Let the grumbling begin. A line begins to form at the owner's door and each grievance is from a full-day worker who feels he has been cheated.

The answer they receive was not what they were looking for but was true all the same. "Friend, I am not being unfair to you. Didn't you agree to work for a denarius? Take your pay and go. I want to give the man hired last the same as I gave you. Don't I have the right to do what I want with my own money? Or are you envious because I am generous?" (Matthew 20:13-15)

The owner first addresses the issue of fairness. He asks the workers if he is being unfair? The answer is an emphatic no. They had agreed to work for a denarius and that is what they were paid.

You have heard the saying "Life's not fair," and that also is a true statement. What we must realize is that we do not live under the law of fairness but under the law of mercy or justice. Fairness has nothing to do with it. We have all said at times "I don't deserve this" and we are right. What we deserve is to go to hell but thank God for mercy and grace found at the cross of Christ! We try to apply fairness to life and we get frustrated because we cannot make it come out right.

Then we attempt to do what C. S. Lewis called "putting God on the docket" and make Him answer for His actions. It may surprise us to know that God does not have to answer for anything He does. He is accountable to no one.

A woman was upset because of a photo taken of her. She went to the photographer and indignantly complained that this picture did not do her justice. The photographer took the picture and looked at her and then again at the picture and replied, "Lady, you don't need justice. What you need is mercy." That is how it is with us. We all stand in need of God's mercy.

We should not be envious of God's generosity with His grace. Everyone loves to talk about grace when they are on the receiving end, but few of us enjoy giving it. We even think we should have a say in who receives God's grace. We must not forget that grace is the great equalizer.

I am writing this chapter the same week that the verdict of George Rivas has been handed down. As the leader of the infamous "Texas Seven" Rivas has been tried for the brutal murder of Irving Police Officer Aubrey Hawkins. Just a few days ago the jury handed down not only a guilty verdict but the death sentence as well. We do not like to think that George Rivas could be a recipient of God's grace, but he could and those are the rules.

As a father of three daughters I see this fairness factor played out almost daily. "You did this for her." "You did not do that for me." "Why are you helping her?" It is interesting that the one I am doing the favor for never questions me.

Would you please stop struggling with fairness and learn to live under grace? No one can be cheated out of an inheritance. It is legally impossible. Whatever the testator decides is what is carried out as the "last will and testament." God's last will and testament came on the cross when His Son gave His life's blood for you and me. He is asking us to receive what has been done for us and to share it with the world.

The happiest people are those who have joyfully received the grace of God at whatever hour it appeared to them. God asks you, "Are you envious because I am generous?"

QUESTIONS

1. Why does God detest our attempts to make life fair?

2. Give a modern day market place setting of the vineyard workers.

3. In what ways does your own daily work environment parallel that of the vineyard workers?

4. Have you ever had an experience similar to that of the workers' disputes, i.e. being on strike, crossing the picket line, attending a volatile union meeting?

5. Why do we have a love/hate relationship with grace?

❁

6. Which group of vineyard workers do you best identify with—the 6:00 A.M. crew, the noon loafers, or the 5:00 P.M. stragglers?

7. How is grace the great equalizer?

8. What does a "merit system" do to the cross?

9. Describe how being envious of God's grace is a contradiction.

10. Do we really care if anyone else receives grace?

Chapter 7

WHAT
WERE YOU
ARGUING
ABOUT ON
THE ROAD?

ROAD Rage. Residing in one of the largest cities in the country, I have definitely seen more than I am looking for. I have witnessed people go from a seemingly mild-mannered person to an accelerator punching, gesturing, challenging, test driving for a spot in the next NASCAR 400 driver. There is nothing like being cut off at the pass to bring out the worst in people. When Jesus was speaking about arguing on the road, I don't think He had this kind of road rage in mind. Neither do I think He was talking about the greatest modern miracle we see in the church today. You know, the kind of arguing on the road for the whole family who is packed in a minivan on the way to Sunday school fighting like cats and dogs. That gives road rage a new definition. When no sooner than they pull into the church parking lot, all arguing ceases and they walk in to say "hello" to the greeters with the biggest smiles ever on their faces. The arguing that was taking place less than two minutes earlier is now a distant memory.

We laugh because it's funny and we laugh because it's true. The same principle holds for the setting in which we find Jesus and the disciples. In order to get the full impact of this question, it is especially important to realize the events that have led up to this conversation. This seeking of pre-eminence has been around since the fall and the followers of Jesus fell prey to it just as we do.

The first event we read about in the ninth chapter of Mark is the transfiguration. Only Peter, James, and John were allowed to witness this event. I think we must all confess that witnessing an event of this magnitude would pump pride in the most humble of servants. I realize that Jesus told these men not to speak about this to anyone, but I doubt if they attempted to hide their strut when they came down from the mountain.

No sooner had they come down from the mountain than they were confronted by a demon-possessed man. Is not that how it always is? We come down from our most spiritual highs only to be met with the lowest of lows. Many of us would rather think about living in the "sweet by and by" rather than the "nasty now and now." How many times have you returned from a spiritually charged meeting only to be faced with a leaky washer, flat tire on your wife's car, sick children, and conflict on the church board? We are more often than not confronted by a demon when we return from the top of the mountain.

What made this demoniac challenge even more difficult was that none of the disciples could do anything about it. Even though they could be given an "A" for effort, it was Jesus who had to step in and cast out the demon. When the disciples asked Him how He had done that, He replied that it could only be accomplished through prayer. Some manuscripts also add the clause "and fasting."

Now fast forward to what the disciples were discussing on the road. After this high-octane interaction with the dark side of the spiritual realm, the most unlikely topic of conversation should have been who is the greatest. Instead of having a discussion about pre-eminence, these men should have been holding a prayer meeting. This group was more concerned with position than true spiritual power. Sound familiar? The question should have been, "Why did we not have the power to cast out this demon?" It is interesting that we are more consumed with being Jesus' right hand man than with overcoming the powers of darkness.

I still believe that Peter, James, and John have a look of pride. They are the three disciples who had seen Jesus transfigured. The other nine disciples had to feel totally left out. When we are feeling our best, this is the time we most wish to exert ourselves and make the case for our own credentials. The followers of Jesus are now having a childish discussion about who is most important. The discussion leads to an argument. The disciples are thinking it is a private argument that Jesus knows nothing about.

Another contributing factor to the discussion on preeminence could have been the fact that Jesus had told His disciples He was going to die. The 12 were possibly wondering who would take over after Jesus died. Whatever the reasons, they were talking about it.

Upon reaching their final destination, Jesus enters the house where they are and asks the question. The setting seems to indicate that the disciples were already in the house. Jesus walks into a room full of tension. Can you remember times this has happened to you? You enter the room and there is a deafening tension in the air. You do not have to ask if anyone has been arguing; you just know it has been happening. People are seated with arms crossed and that glazed look in their eyes. The conversation they thought was private is just about to become public.

There were probably a couple of reactions to Jesus' question. The first reaction was surprise. His followers were caught off guard by the question. These men were definitely ticked off by Jesus. They had to be thinking, "How in the world did He know all we were talking about?"

The second reaction was shame. The shame of the disciples was made obvious by their silence. These men had nothing to say. Jesus really knew how to nail people. No one wanted to confess to his pride. Isn't it interesting that the very thing that causes us to sin keeps us from confessing it? At this point, it was quieter than a tomb.

It is now time for Jesus to take control of the situation. This is a teachable moment. Everyone is ready to listen. School is in session. Listen to what the master teacher has to say. Let's be truthful, we all need a lesson in Humility 101.

Jesus takes a seat and begins to teach. He says, "Guys, you have it all wrong." One of the first things a child learns to say is "I had it first!" No one likes waiting in line. Jesus is teaching that pre-eminence can never be our motivator. He is trying to teach the principle of servant leadership. Pride is a lousy method to influence others. Very few people want to follow an arrogant, obnoxious person. Jesus was teaching that we must prefer others before ourselves.

You must remember the group of people Jesus is talking to here. These 12 men were not crazy about each other.

They did not stand around the campfire holding hands and singing "Kum Ba Ya." They were not known for their warm fuzzies and group hugs. Most of the time they did not even like each other. You know, just like people in your church; everyone likes to be recognized. The rub comes, though, when recognition becomes our ultimate goal.

As Jesus is attempting to make His point, He uses the most loved of all God's creation—a child. Children are the greatest things God ever made. I love children. They're so trusting, innocent, sweet, and energetic. Jesus deeply loved children and used them more than once to make a point— this time to drive home the lesson of humility.

I do not know the exact age of the child Jesus uses here. I'm thinking somewhere between four to seven years old, old enough to stand still for Jesus to make His point and yet small enough for Him to hold in His arms. He spoke of our need to welcome children. I can tell you a lot about a person based on how he relates to children. Show me some- one who will get down in the floor and play with children and I'll show you someone God can use.

Jesus was making His disciples know there was no need to fight about pre-eminence. They just needed to be con- cerned with serving one another. I have never seen a greater need for servant leadership than exists in the church today.

I loved Jerry Clower. His homespun clean humor was and still is a rare commodity. I saw him in a restaurant just a few months before he died. I deeply regret that I did not go speak to him and share with him what a blessing he had

❧

been to me. A man I pastor recently gave me a book that Jerry Clower wrote entitled *Life Ever Laughter*. This book tells of Jerry Clower's life and has many of his funny stories sprinkled throughout.

There is one picture in this book that caught my attention. Jerry Clower is standing next to a framed saying that he saw in a pharmacy in McComb, Mississippi. He admired it so much that the pharmacist gave it to him. The plaque is inscribed, "There is no limit to what can be done when it does not matter who gets the credit." Think of how that philosophy could turn your world upside down. If we in the church could only capture this attitude, imagine how we could grow!

Just remember, the kingdom belongs to a child. The world needs to stop seeing how we are fighting and start seeing our service. No one wants to be in a place where there is fighting. Everyone wants to be where there is love and concern. What were you fighting about on the road?

QUESTIONS
1. Why did Jesus only allow Peter, James, and John to see His transfiguration?

2. Did the transfiguration have the desired effect Jesus had hoped for upon these men?

3. Why are we so afraid of not receiving proper recognition?

4. Is this the only time the disciples had the discussion of who would be the greatest?

5. Why do you think this story kept repeating itself?

6. What lesson was Jesus trying to teach the disciples from the exorcism of the demon?

7. After reading this story, why do we still choose pre-eminence over prayer?

8. In what ways does a child still teach us about humility?

9. How long do you think it took the disciples to get it?

10. What is the difference in being "childish" and having "child like faith"?

HAVEN'T YOU
READ . . .
THE TWO
WILL BECOME
ONE FLESH.

❧

"HOW is Walt doing?" I asked Mandy. "I don't know," she replied. "We divorced over three years ago and I have not seen him since." I was not prepared for such a brusque response.

Though the names have been changed, this was an actual incident at my first high school reunion. I learned a lesson then. I never ask anyone about his or her spouse unless I have recently seen the spouse standing right next to him or her.

These were two kids I had gone to school with for many years. I had attended their wedding while home on break from college. What had happened?

The tragedy is that this story plays out all too often. We have all probably been caught with our foot hanging out our mouth at one time or another when asking someone about their spouse.

As you have probably already figured out, this chapter is going to deal with the subject of divorce. Divorce was once a hot topic in society as well as in the church culture, but unfortunately, has been relegated to the back of the bus. So many other issues seem to take precedence over the sanctity of marriage and the preservation of the home.

The most telling statistic in recent years is one from George Barna that showed divorce is just as common among those who are part of the church as those who are outside the church community. Something is definitely wrong in the church.

Divorce has become so widely accepted in our culture that we are almost expected to trade our mates every five years just as we do our automobiles. Many people replace their mate with "a newer model."

If you have been divorced, please do not stop reading this chapter. My purpose in writing on this subject is not to condemn, but rather to offer hope and healing. Divorce is not the "unforgivable sin," though it is a sin. Let me make clear that there can be life after divorce.

The purpose of this chapter is "preventative maintenance." If you are currently contemplating a divorce or face this decision later down the road, please consider what you are about to do. Those who are considering divorce are on the verge of bringing destruction to many lives around them.

Let's hop into the time machine and see what was going on in Jesus' day that prompted such a question. What was the pulse of first century family life especially among adherents of the Jewish religion?

It is interesting to note that Jesus was asked this question toward the end of His earthly ministry. This narrative occurred just prior to Passion Week. The spiritual Gestapo, the Pharisees, were the ones to ask this question. Divorce seemed to be a fairly hot topic also during the days of Jesus.

The good old Pharisees! I love the little song for a child that says, "I just want to be a sheep." One line says, "I don't want to be a Pharisee, 'cause they're just not fair, you see." These guys were always trying to bend the rules.

There were several prevailing schools of thought concerning divorce from different rabbinical sources. (Richard Foster gives an excellent explanation of this in *Money, Sex and Power.*)

When Jesus was asked the question, "Is it lawful for a man to divorce his wife for any and every reason?" (Matthew 19:3), that is exactly what they meant. We know that these men never had pure motives when they were questioning Jesus.

Matthew tells us it was the usual "testing" question. You know, the "I'll take divorce for $500, Alex" type of question.

There is no doubt, though, that they were wanting Jesus to give His stamp of approval on the divorce practices of their day.

The use of divorce had become so common that men were literally divorcing their wives for burning the biscuits. It was legal and the women had no say in it whatsoever. Jesus Christ did more for women's rights than any man that ever lived. I actually think Jesus was anticipating this question like Barry Bonds waiting on a big fat curve ball with the count 2-1. He was on this question like white on rice.

The beauty of Jesus' style of apologetics is again displayed as He answers a question with a question. He is now asking men who possibly have memorized the Pentateuch if they have read it. Hello! Jesus refers to a verse in Genesis 2, where God begins to give His blueprint for marriage. "Haven't you read," he replied, "that at the beginning the

Creator 'made them male and female,' and said 'For this reason, a man will leave his father and mother and be united to his wife, and the two will become one flesh'? So, they are no longer two, but one. Therefore what God has joined together, let man not separate" (Matthew 19:4-6).

It is God's intention for a marriage to last. It is time we stopped offering excuses and start repenting. Some believers treat divorce like a new discovery in the abuse of grace.

The Pharisees were not content with this answer from Jesus, so they pressed the issue. "Why then," they asked, "did Moses command that a man give his wife a certificate of divorce and send her away?" (Matthew 19:7). These men did not like what they heard. They wanted to continue to treat women like property and not as someone whom God intended to be "one" with them.

The experts of the law are now trying to pit Jesus against Moses. I personally think Moses would have really gotten hot about this. What they are saying to Jesus is, "If divorce is such a bad thing, then why did Moses allow it?" Surely, Jesus, You would not accuse Moses of being soft on the Law! Just look at what Jesus had to say next.

Jesus replied, "Moses permitted you to divorce your wives because your hearts were hard. But it was not this way from the beginning" (Matthew 19:8). Jesus was saying that what God the Father had said about marriage in Genesis superceded what Moses later wrote in the law. The reason Moses was driven to permit divorce was because of hardness of the heart. Just as the hardening of the arteries is dan-

꧁

gerous to our physical health, so is the hardening of our hearts to our spiritual health.

If you are considering divorce from your mate without validity, your heart is already starting to harden and you need to repent right now. Ask God to restore your love for your mate. Ask God to melt your cold heart and take out that stony heart and put in a heart of flesh.

Two people on fire for Jesus do not get divorced. One or both suffer from hardness of the heart. I understand that divorce at times is unavoidable, but many divorces are unnecessary. God simply does not buy this "I am just not happy any more" garbage.

How many homes have been demolished because passions were not controlled, unforgiveness began to dominate a relationship and people simply could not get past themselves? If you are in the divorce mode, I urge you to reconsider before it is too late.

We do not need revival in our churches nearly as much as we need revival in our homes. I guarantee you I will go home tonight and hug my sweet wife and tell her how much I love her.

When you begin to be pulled apart, remember the words of Jesus, "Haven't you read . . . the two will become one flesh?" No one can heal a marriage like Jesus.

QUESTIONS

1. Under what circumstances is divorce justified?

2. How "concerned" were the Pharisees about the condition of the home?

3. Is happiness the most important factor in a marital relationship? Explain your answer.

4. How did culture's view of women add to the divorce epidemic of the first century?

5. Discuss the divorced people with whom Jesus came in contact. What was His attitude toward them?

6. What kind of stance should the church take concerning divorce?

7. What factors contribute to the hardening of the heart?

8. What is the best way to prevent a divorce from happening?

9. Did Jesus condemn divorce with His answer or endorse it?

10. What are some ways culture is weakened by divorce?

CHAPTER

9

JUDAS,
DO YOU
BETRAY
THE SON
OF MAN
WITH A KISS.?

❧

BENEDICT Arnold, Brutus, Judas Iscariot. These names are synonymous with betrayal. They are never used in a complimentary way. I have yet to hear of someone naming his or her son Judas in the past 2,000 years. If they did, we would think they were twisted. Anyone familiar with United States history cannot hear the name Benedict Arnold without a hollow feeling of mistrust sweep over him or her.

In more recent times we equate betrayal with such names as Robert Hansen and John Walker Lindh. We despise those who sell out their country, a friendship, or a worthy cause for which millions have died. Just remember, however, the betrayer, though vile to us, is a hero to others.

I will have to say by the grace of God that I am yet to be the victim of a harsh betrayal. I am sure most of us have fallen victim to the milder betrayals of life, but I write this chapter based more on objectivity than personal experience. There is little doubt, though, that some of you will read this chapter while simultaneously going through the corridors of your memory and reliving some painful times of betrayal. Betrayal can manifest itself in just about any situation. One co-worker can tell another co-worker they are really hoping for a promotion only to be called to a meeting the next week to see that very person receive the promotion. Betrayal is so much a part of politics that it seems to be accepted as the norm, and many marriages end in divorce as a result of betrayal.

❧

Most of you reading this book have a desire to be like Jesus (the rest of you we hope to win over). Sometimes I wonder how much we really want to be like Jesus. One of my favorite verses is Philippians 3:10, "That I may know Him and the power of His resurrection, and the fellowship of His sufferings, being made conformable unto His death." I think we all start out with big guns on this verse when we talk about "resurrection power," but our enthusiasm soon gives way when "the fellowship of His sufferings" begins to kick in. Do we really want to know Jesus? Do we really want to be like Jesus? More on the practical side, do we want to experience what Jesus did in order to be more like Him? Father God, give us the courage and grace to say yes to these questions.

I have to confess when I began to prepare mentally to write this chapter, I was blindsided by the Holy Spirit. He reminded me of my senior football season when I came back after several weeks out due to an injury. At the end of one of the game's first plays, my rib cage was greeted by a helmet.

I was standing around and was not yet "battle ready." I can assure you that incident did not repeat itself for the rest of the season.

In the same way, the Holy Spirit knocked me to the floor as I considered the question of betrayal. What jolted me was the Holy Spirit bringing to light my own pride and arrogance in thinking that I should be exempt from betrayal. In thinking that, I was considering myself to be better plain# CHAPTER 9

✦

than Jesus! How is it that we continue to allow our own humanity along with the enemy to deceive us into thinking that we are above going through the same trials of life that Jesus did? How else are we to become more like Him and assimilate into the 'fellowship of His sufferings"?

Let's look at the man known as Judas Iscariot. There were actually two disciples known as Judas, but Judas Iscariot stands out in both lists for two reasons. He is always listed last and he is denoted as the betrayer. The name Iscariot indicates he was from Kerioth, which was 12 miles from Hebron, where David reigned his first seven years as king.

Judas was the only disciple who was not from Galilee. He was from Judea with his sights set high. He loved the spotlight and power he had as the treasurer among the disciples. The person who holds the purse strings is always one to be reckoned with. When there was so much upheaval over the 2000 presidential election, someone from Japan said it really didn't matter who was in the White House as long as Alan Greenspan was in charge of the interest rate.

To say that Judas was ambitious is an understatement. He was following Jesus for all the wrong reasons. Judas expected Jesus to come in and set up a powerful political kingdom, which was never on Jesus' agenda.

The earthly ministry of Jesus can be broken down into three different segments.

The first year was the year of *inauguration.* This is when Jesus is literally introduced to the world. The second year

was the year of *popularity*. This was when everybody wanted a part of Jesus. He could not go anywhere without being
mobbed. At this juncture, I think Judas is having the time
of his life. Jesus is on the verge of world domination and
there is already talk of making Him a king. Oh sure, He has
some opponents, but they cannot make anything derogato-
ry stick. Jesus is going to be king and Judas the secretary of
the treasury. He might even make secretary of state or vice-
president if he can jockey into position around Peter,
James, and John.

The third year of Jesus' ministry brought a rude awak-
ening to Judas. This year is known as the year of *opposition*
and things start to get ugly. Jesus begins to talk more and
more about dying on a cross. His opponents seem more
determined to put Him away. Worst of all, Jesus does not
seem to care! Judas is not about to be associated with a loser
who does not put up a fight. His world is quickly unravel-
ing.

This is when Judas makes what he feels is an extremely
shrewd political move. He betrays Jesus for about $3,000
(thirty pieces of silver in those days). Judas did not realize
he was making the biggest mistake of his life. He was so
smug and proud of himself. When it came to covering your
back, Judas could have written the book. I do not know
why God allowed this scene to play out like it did. Don't
ever think that Judas was without a choice, and was just
some pawn on the big universal chessboard. He had a
choice. Here are some things I believe God wants us to

CHAPTER 9

❦

learn from this: Jesus never related to Judas any differently than He did to the rest of the disciples. The disciples were oblivious of the betrayal up until the end. Even when they were told that one of you will betray me, they did not know who Jesus was talking about. Do you not think that Jesus could have tipped His hand? Jesus never stopped reaching out to Judas. At the last supper when the betrayal was announced, Jesus dipped a piece of bread into a bowl and offered it to Judas. This was Jesus' final time to reach out to Judas and say, "You do not have to do this." Judas refused and it was then that the devil entered into him. Jesus handled the betrayal with grace and dignity. It is evident that God wants us to know from this narrative that betrayal is a part of life. One of the 12 select members of Jesus' special forces sold Him out. Who is to say it will not happen to us? The crucial question here is not will we be betrayed, but how will we handle betrayal? Look at how in control Jesus was when Judas betrayed Him, and all hell literally breaks loose as the demonic forces of Satan get their hands on the Son of God.

Jesus never loses His cool. There is none of this "How could you do this to me?" wallowing going on. Jesus simply asks, "Judas are you betraying the son of man with a kiss?" (Luke 22:48)

When betrayal hits us, we are so busy playing the victim and getting a mourning section together, we fail to see what God is trying to accomplish through us. Jesus accepted the betrayal as part of God's sovereign plan.

What happened as a result of the betrayal? Jesus is arrested and tried. He is eventually found guilty of treason and is executed on a cross. He is laid to rest in a borrowed tomb and comes out on the third day as our resurrected Lord!

Judas sees his sin and goes to the wrong people for forgiveness. He returns the money and goes out and commits suicide. Which ending would you choose? When we show grace to those who are 'sticking it to us,' I am sure we are perceived as some idiot who has not a clue of what is happening. It is certain that Judas must have thought he was getting one over on Jesus. Who cares?

Judas now only serves as an object lesson of a loser who betrayed Jesus. Jesus' name is spoken around the clock, around the world. He is our Lord, our Savior, our coming King.

So, I ask you, what will it take for you to sell out Jesus? Is there anything worth it?

*Q*UESTIONS

   1. When and to whom is the betrayer a hero?

   2. Name other people in Scripture who were known as betrayers.

3. Why do you think God chose betrayal as the major factor in the crucifixion story?

4. Describe a time you have felt betrayed.

5. What other sins was Judas guilty of?

6. What is the betrayal kiss symbolic of?

7. Was it possible for Judas to be forgiven?

3. What was the difference in Judas' betrayal and Peter's denial?

9. Why didn't the disciples physically restrain Judas?

CHAPTER
10

WHO
DO PEOPLE
SAY THE
SON OF MAN
IS?

SEVERAL years ago an ad featured a famous tennis star who made the statement "Image is everything." Our culture has to be the most "image conscious" of all time. All of this consciousness is media driven and rarely portrays the actual person. We are led to think what people or their promoters want us to think about them.

Can you imagine electing a president without the aid of the electronic media? Believe it or not, this nation elected more than 30 presidents in a pre-television era. The first televised presidential debate was not until 1960 between John F. Kennedy and Richard Nixon. We have only had the advantage of televised presidential campaigns for less than 50 years.

Jesus had no such help in His day, therefore people had to make up their minds about Jesus based on what they saw with their own eyes. It is ludicrous to think someone could become as well known as Jesus without an agent, an image consultant, or a good speechwriter.

For Jesus even to ask this question displays both tremendous courage and self-assurance. How many times have you gone around taking surveys on what people are saying about you? This is open to debate, but I believe Jesus knew the answer to every question He asked. It is quite clear then that He always asked questions to make people think and make His point.

Jesus was nearing the end of His earthly ministry when He asked: "Who do people say the Son of man is?" Jesus already knew who He was but He wanted the disciples to know who He was. It was imperative for the disciples to have the correct perception of Jesus before He turned His earthly ministry over to them. They needed to know who the center of their message was and where their power came from. Without a clear understanding of Jesus, it is virtually impossible to make any kind of impact for Him.

Jesus was about to give a quick lesson in Christology and make the point that mistaken identity can lead to mass confusion. The masses today are still in confusion about who Jesus is. That should not surprise us as we have full knowledge about Jesus' mistaken identity during the actual time that he lived!

First, let's consider the answer to Jesus' question. One of the primary rules of biblical interpretation is first to conclude what the person was saying in his time and to his culture. Jesus simply asked the disciples who people were saying He was.

Their answers varied. They replied, "Some say John the Baptist; others say Elijah; and still others, Jeremiah or one of the prophets" (Matthew 16:14). The disciples were not necessarily confused themselves about who Jesus was, they were merely reporting what others were saying.

It is interesting that they mentioned three different men who had lived in completely different times. A fourth possibility was mentioned; Jesus might be one of the prophets. Many people still believe that Jesus was just a prophet. The first name mentioned was John the Baptist. John had been the forerunner of Jesus and was also His cousin. He was six

❧

months older than Jesus and had only been dead for a short time. For Jesus to have been called John the Baptist would have meant several things.

The first was that John had been resurrected. This was not very likely. The second hurdle would be to explain how Jesus and John had co-existed. It was John who baptized Jesus and proclaimed Him to be the Lamb of God who takes away the sin of the world. This would have been virtually impossible and by far the least likely possibility.

The second possibility given was Elijah who was an interesting choice for several reasons. Elijah had lived around 850 B.C. and was the Old Testament counterpart to John the Baptist. In fact, it was said that John the Baptist had come in the spirit of Elijah. To say that Elijah had been resurrected comes with a twist because no one actually saw Elijah die. He was carried into the heavens in a chariot of fire. Because of this, many Jews looked for him to return and thought Jesus had fulfilled this expectation.

The last name given was intriguing because it was Jeremiah, the weeping prophet. One of the reasons Jeremiah wept was because he was one of the most unsuccessful prophets on record. He was even known as "Death and Destruction." He began his ministry around 600 B.C. and was in Jerusalem to witness its fall in 586 B.C. Jeremiah wrote the book of Lamentations as he mourned the fall of Jerusalem. Interestingly enough, Jesus quoted Jeremiah more than any other prophet.

✽

The final possibility given was "one of the prophets." I believe this was done in case the people had missed on the first three choices that they had. It is incredible how the movement to make Jesus totally generic began while He was still alive. The enemy loves for Jesus just to be lumped together with a lot of great men who have made an impact for the kingdom.

This chapter ends here, but the thought continues in the next one.

QUESTIONS

1. Was Jesus ever concerned about His image?

2. Why was there confusion about Jesus while He was on earth?

3. When people hear the name "Jesus" today, does the image flash positive or negative?

❧

4. Were the disciples in touch with mainstream culture, or just Jewish culture?

5. Why would anyone think Jesus was John the Baptist, Elijah, or Jeremiah?

6. Is there more confusion about Jesus today than in the first century?

7. What would be the reason that Jesus referred to Himself as the "Son of man" in this discourse?

❧

8. Do you think the disciples answered Jesus' question correctly?

9. Is there anything significant about where Jesus was when He asked this question?

10. What would be the answer to this question if it were asked today?

WHO
DO YOU
SAY I
AM

I JUST finished talking to a friend on the phone. He is old enough to be my father, but he has been a source of support and encouragement to me. I pastored this man and his wife several years back while in Oklahoma.

I called Harold today because his wife, Alveta, is dying. She probably will not live till the end of this week. We talked about the past, the present, and the future.

The future for a child of God is bright! When someone is nearing the end of a life that has been lived for Jesus, faith begins to give way to sight. As I prayed with Harold over the phone, I said, "This is what our faith is all about." It is having the faith to live, but more importantly, having the faith to die that really matters.

This is really what Jesus was talking about when He asked the question, "Who do you say I am?" Do you believe in me? Do you know I am the way, the truth, and the life?

You will notice that He began this discourse in a very general way by asking, "Who do people say the Son of man is?" (Matthew 16:13b). In the previous chapter we discussed how Jesus was taking a survey of the general public. It is so much easier to communicate in general terms rather than more specific ones. It is much easier to say "We love you," than to say "I love you."

Jesus never lets life stay generalized. He always shoots for the heart. This is never proven with more clarity than in this passage from Matthew 16. After Jesus asks what the people are saying and after getting the typical response, He turned His attention to the disciples as solitary human beings and asked "What about you?" (Matthew 16:15a). The degree of difficulty in making a statement becomes much greater when the statement is "I say," instead of "We say."

An interesting paradigm shift in our culture is actually paradoxical in nature. Personal freedom and individuality are more treasured than ever before. They are seen as a right rather than a privilege. On the other hand, personal responsibility and accountability are shirked and avoided more than at any other time in our history. We are constantly hit with a verbal barrage exclaiming, "I want to live my life however I please, but pass the check to the end of the table when it comes time to pay for the consequences of my actions." Never before has corporate living been so despised except when it comes to shared responsibilities for actions taken.

Jesus promotes individual accountability. He died on the cross so we would not have to depend on any human entity to get us to Heaven. No one can stop you from making a conscious decision to follow Jesus. That was the point He was trying to make when He said, "But what about you?" Jesus was bringing the conversation around to a personal response. We have to make a personal decision for Christ. You can receive Jesus at a mass evangelism event along with many other people but He must still save you personally. It is a very personal decision that is made extremely public.

❧

My wife and I have a personal and intimate relationship. We nevertheless pledged our love to one another in a very public wedding ceremony on December 18, 1982.

Jesus does not expect our salvation to be a private matter. He died for us publicly. We must come to Him publicly.

Jesus was definitely forcing the disciples' hand when He asked them who they professed Him to be. He was getting to the heart of the matter to see if they really believed in Him. At this juncture, Peter stepped to the plate and hit a home run. Peter struck out a lot (as we can well see later in this chapter), but this is one time he knocked the ball out of the park. For once, he actually said what Jesus wanted to hear. We know that Peter was always swift to speak and slow to listen. We were not there to know if there was much of a pause between Jesus' question and Peter's response. Whether or not there was, we know this—Peter was the only one with the guts to say anything.

Peter actually said, "You are the Christ, the Son of the living God" (Matthew 16:16). This was the correct answer and it was also the first time it was given. The previous opinions given about Jesus had all been wrong. We do not live our lives by a faith based on opinions, but rather by a faith built on truth.

There are two extremely popular schools of thought that are archenemies of the gospel message. One is that Jesus was not and is not the Son of God. This teaching falls in line with the answers we discussed in the former chapter.

Just as in the time of Jesus, people are confused about who
He is. As was true in the first century, Jesus is still believed
to be "one of the prophets." Others say He was a great
teacher who died for what He believed. Others say He was
a martyr on which the Christian faith is built. In all of this
the divinity of Jesus is denied. When Peter said, "You are
the Son of the living God," he was ascribing divinity to
Jesus. It would be impossible to be the Son of God without
being divine yourself. A definite article is used here. Jesus is
not *a* son of God, but *the* Son of God.

Another prevailing school of thought that is making
inroads into the church is universalism. Universalism teach-
es that everyone will eventually make it to Heaven regardless of what they believe about Jesus. This totally cuts across
the grain of the message that proclaims Jesus to be the only
way to God. Without Him, there is no salvation.

What about you? Have you come to the cross? The cross
is a symbol of death. Jesus died there to save us from our
sins. He bled so we could be redeemed and find forgiveness
by having our sinful hearts made clean by His blood.

To have Jesus as your Lord and Savior, you must first
repent of your sins.

Repentance means to change your mind, to be sorry for
your sins and not just sorry you were caught. Salvation is
impossible without repentance. Repentance never needs to
stop being a part of the believer's life.

You must accept what Jesus did on the cross as your only
hope of salvation and eternal life. You must also believe that

God raised Him from the dead and confess Him as Lord and Savior.

Jesus is the only way!

There is what I call, for lack of a better term, an "UnJesusness" in our churches. We preach biblical history. We preach social issues, we preach our church and denomination, but Paul said we are to make nothing known except "Jesus Christ and Him crucified" (1 Corinthians 2:2).

You can talk about God, you can discuss theology and philosophy, you can debate the origin of the cosmos, but when the name of Jesus comes into the conversation everything changes. Hell stands at attention when the name of Jesus is mentioned. May we never be afraid to speak His name!

Jesus asks each of us, "Who do you say I am?" Everything in this life and the next one depends on our answer.

QUESTIONS

1. Why is universalism becoming so popular?

2. How does believing in Jesus as "the way" make you appear intolerant?

3. Why do so many world religions at least make some reference to Jesus?

4. What is the direct link from a "watered down" gospel to the growth in nominal Christianity?

5. Why is it so important to keep our message Christ centered?

✦

6. Why was it so important for the disciples to know who Jesus was?

7. Discuss whether or not you think Peter was the only disciple that knew who Jesus was.

8. How dangerous is it to be wrong about Jesus?

CHAPTER 12

COULD
YOU MEN
NOT KEEP
WATCH WITH
ME ONE
HOUR?

SUMMERTIME—I love it. Growing up in rural Arkansas brings so many pleasant memories of summer. Going swimming in one of my favorite creeks, fresh fish dinners cooked out on an open flame, little league baseball, Fourth of July picnics, and my favorite—homemade ice cream. Summer is still not summer until I have consumed a heaping bowl of ice cream fresh from the ice cream maker. My personal choice is banana.

Mom would not settle for anything less than a crank model ice cream freezer, which she said made the ice cream taste better, and I believe she was right. I learned several lessons while cranking ice cream for many hours of my life. One lesson I learned was that you need a strong arm for cranking ice cream. Cranking out ice cream is not for wimps. The second one that really stuck with me was the tremendous amount of patience involved in letting the ingredients freeze in order to have ice cream. The third lesson was that the cranking got harder with each revolution, more resistance was continually offered.

Oh, but it was worth the wait! The taste of fresh banana ice cream was an exquisite reward. The thought of it makes my mouth water even now. I am thankful for the lessons learned around that old ice cream freezer. Especially the one on patience.

Jesus was emphasizing the power of patience in this final question we will look at. I believe with this question Jesus was attempting to convey the tremendous value of watchful patience.

One of my hallmark Bible verses that I have taught my daughters is Proverbs 16:32 which says, "Better a patient man than a warrior, a man who controls his temper than one who takes a city." I believe patience is one of the most undersold disciplines in the life of a believer. We often hear the saying "To the victor goes the spoils," which I think should be changed to "To the patient go the spoils."

The question under consideration was asked at one of the most intense moments in the life of Jesus. Jesus asked this question just moments before being arrested, which eventually led to His crucifixion.

Let us set the scene in Gethsemane. Jesus went with His disciples to this garden to pray. It appears that the 11 were with Him. He first addresses the entire group by saying, "Sit here while I go over there and pray" (Matthew 26:36). Then He took Peter, James, and John with Him and began to be "sorrowful and troubled." Verse 38 says; "Then He said to them, My soul is overwhelmed with sorrow to the point of death. Stay here and keep watch with me." Jesus was trying to impress upon His three inner circle followers the distress He was feeling. Have you ever tried to express to someone the despair you were experiencing only to have it fall on deaf ears? Jesus knows how you feel.

Jesus was saying, "I need you guys to wait it out with me. I need some prayer support and concern. Is that too much to ask?" I am afraid it was too much to ask the disciples and many times it is also too much to ask of us today.

လာ

As Jesus begins to put distance between Himself and the disciples, He falls on His face in agony of spirit and starts to pray. The trauma of the cross must have been gut wrenching. This is where Jesus prays the familiar words; "Not my will, but Thine be done." Jesus, here, totally surrenders His will to the will of the Father.

As Jesus is making the most important decision in His life, as well as ours—the decision to die for our sins—what do you think the disciples are doing? They are sleeping! Luke tells us that Jesus was in such a tightly wound emotional condition that He actually sweated blood. What a picture of Jesus and the church today. He is fervently interceding while we kick back and take a nap.

Jesus comes back to find the disciples sleeping and asks the convicting question, "Could you men not keep watch with me one hour?" (Matthew 26:40b). This question was actually directed to Peter. I believe Jesus pointed the question toward Peter because of the enormous temptation that Peter was about to undergo. Peter needed to be praying instead of sleeping.

These men had been through an exhausting week. Passion week had taken its toll and they could no longer keep their eyes open. Jesus just needed one hour but they could not give it to Him.

One hour can change your life. Spending an hour a day with Jesus can change your entire perspective and revitalize you spiritually. To give daily time to Jesus requires the discipline of patience. We daily think that our agendas are so important that they deserve to be charged with the fury of a rhinoceros. We dive so quickly into our day without taking the time to "wait upon the Lord" and seek His face in prayer. People jump the gun much more often than waiting too long.

People who are patient are criticized by those less mature as being lazy, indecisive, and not aggressive enough. Listen, Jesus never had an indecisive moment in His life. He always knew where He was going and had the patience to see it come about.

In asking us to watch and pray, Jesus also said the hour is near. In that particular context, He was saying that His time to be betrayed and arrested was upon them. In a more relevant sense, Jesus is telling us that He is coming back and expects to find us prayerfully watching for Him.

Are you keeping watch? Are you tired of waiting on Jesus? Blessed is the man whom He finds watching. We have to pray and we have to watch. Both go hand in hand.

Are you spending time daily with Jesus? Do you daily confess with your mouth, "Jesus Christ is coming back?" Do not go to sleep! Stay prayed up as you watch for Jesus to come. Doing that can change your life. So I ask, what are you waiting for?

CHAPTER 12

❦

QUESTIONS

1. Why did Jesus emphasize prayer so much?

2. Can you share a time when you were called to prayer when it was extremely inconvenient?

3. What does this narrative teach about lost opportunities to pray?

4. Why is patience such an undersold discipline in the life of a believer?

5. What does impatience tell about our spiritual maturation?

6. Why is it so difficult to live in the light of Christ's return?

7. In what ways does time alone with God revolutionize your life?

8. Does Jesus expect us to pray every day? Explain your answer.

❧

9. How does Jesus want us to watch and pray? How should this discipline be reflected in the life of a believer?

10. Jesus was overwhelmed by the urgency of the moment while the disciples slept. How does this parallel the activity of the church today?